DECADES OF THE 20th CENTURY

IN COLOR

THE 1900s

FROM TEDDY ROOSEVELT TO FLYING MACHINES   REVISED EDITION

STEPHEN FEINSTEIN

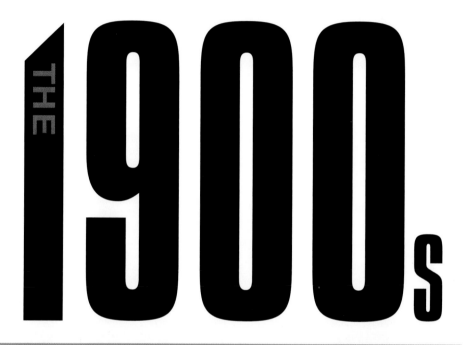

Library of Congress Cataloging-in-Publication Data

Feinstein, Stephen.
   The 1900s from Teddy Roosevelt to flying machines / Stephen Feinstein.— Rev. ed.
      p. cm. — (Decades of the 20th century in color)
   Includes index.
   ISBN 0-7660-2630-2
   1. United States—Civilization—1865–1918—Juvenile literature. 2. Nineteen hundreds (Decade)—Juvenile literature. I. Title. II. Series: Feinstein, Stephen. Decades of the 20th century in color.
E169.1.F353 2006
973.91'1—dc22

                                2005019847

Printed in the United States of America

10 9 8 7 6 5 4 3 2 1

To Our Readers: We have done our best to make sure all Internet Addresses in this book were active and appropriate when we went to press. However, the author and the publisher have no control over and assume no liability for the material available on those Internet sites or on other Web sites they may link to. Any comments or suggestions can be sent by e-mail to comments@enslow.com or to the address on the back cover.

Illustration Credits: AP/Wide World Photos, pp. 13 (top), 46–47, 51; Bert Randolph Sugar, *The Great Baseball Players from McGraw to Mantle* (Mineola, N.Y.: Dover Publications, Inc., 1997), p. 34; Colonel G. W. Townsend, *Our Martyred President: Memorial Life of William McKinley* (Washington, D.C.: Memorial Publishing Company, 1901), p. 38; Corel Corporation, pp. 13 (inset), 19, 20 (right), 28, 53 (top background), 58; Enslow Publishers, Inc., pp. 16 (inset), 17, 57; Everett Collection, Inc., pp. 25, 56; French Archives, p. 54; Hayward Cirker, ed., *Old-Time Advertising Cards* (New York: Dover Publications, Inc., 1989), pp. 7, 12, 15 (inset); JoAnne Olian, ed., *Everyday Fashions 1909–1920 As Pictured in Sears Catalogs* (New York: Dover Publications, Inc., 1995), pp. 18, 20 (left), 21; Jupiterimages Corporation, pp. 35, 55; Library of Congress, pp. 6, 8, 10, 11 (top right), 14 (bottom), 14–15 (top), 16 (top), 22, 26, 27, 29, 30, 32–33, 48–49 (top), 49 (bottom); National Archives, p. 4; Reproduced from the *Dictionary of American Portraits*, Published by Dover Publications, Inc., 1967, pp. 11 (top left), 31, 40, 41, 52, 53 (inset); Russian State Archive, p. 48 (inset); Sagamore Hill National Historic Site, pp. 36, 39, 42, 44; Theodore Roosevelt Collection, Harvard College Library, p. 43; U.S. Geological Survey, p. 24; Willis J. Abbot, *Panama and the Canal: In Pictures and Prose* (London: Syndicate Publishing Company, 1913), p. 45; Wright State University, p. 50.

All interior collages composed by Enslow Publishers, Inc. Images used are courtesy of the previously credited rights holders.

Cover Illustrations: AP/Wide World Photos; Corel Corporation; Enslow Publishers, Inc.; Hayward Cirker, ed., *Old-Time Advertising Cards* (New York: Dover Publications, Inc., 1989); Library of Congress; Sagamore Hill National Historic Site.

Enslow Publishers, Inc.
40 Industrial Road
Box 398
Berkeley Heights, NJ 07922
USA

http://www.enslow.com

Contents

By the time the twentieth century began, people had been moving—across the continent to the West and to America from foreign countries—for years. But the sight of wagon trains moving westward would soon be completely replaced by motor-driven automobiles and even airplanes.

Introduction

The year 1900 marked a new beginning. During the nineteenth century, America had grown from a small group of states on the East Coast to a mighty nation spanning the continent from ocean to ocean. The nation had survived a terrible civil war, emerging stronger and better. Countless pioneers made the often dangerous overland trek to the West in covered wagons. America's reputation as a land of opportunity continued to grow at the turn of the twentieth century. Millions of people from around the world, filled with hopes and dreams for a better life, packed their bags and headed to America.

Americans looked to the future with confidence. It seemed that the United States was about to join the ranks of other great powers such as Great Britain and France. The nation was about to take its place as a major player on the world stage.

In 1900, about 60 percent of Americans still lived in rural areas, mainly on farms. To get to town, they had to hitch up a horse to a buggy. Soon, many Americans would toss away their buggy whips and drive around in their new horseless carriages—cars. Few would have believed that within just a few years, people would travel through the air in flying machines.

The Promised Land Beckons

A massive wave of immigration began around 1890. It continued during the first decade of the 1900s. Almost 9 million men, women, and children arrived in the United States between 1900 and 1910. They came in search of a better life.

America was in the midst of transforming from a nation of farms, shops, and mills into a booming industrial power with factories that needed workers. Major cities, especially in the Northeast and Midwest, bustled with the energy of newly arrived immigrants. Adding to the exploding population of cities were hundreds of thousands of native-born, rural American migrants, who were drawn to the cities for the

Growing factories were eager to have as many new employees as possible—including women (left), who moved into the workforce steadily through the 1900s. By 1910, nearly one seventh of America's population was foreign born, thanks to a huge wave of immigration (opposite). New York City had more Italians than Rome, more Jews than Warsaw, and more Irish than Dublin.

same reasons as foreign immigrants—better economic opportunities. In 1900, only 40 percent of America's nearly 76 million people lived in urban areas. By the end of the decade, 45 percent of the nation's population, which had grown to almost 92 million, lived in cities. The day would soon come when America's urban population would outnumber the rural population.

A Gentlemen's Agreement

The majority of immigrants arriving in the United States during the 1900s were from eastern, central, and southern Europe. A smaller number of Asian immigrants from China and Japan settled in the West, mainly in California. As more immigrants arrived, growing numbers of native-born Americans began

Although Japanese workers were generally devoted and skillful, like these Japanese farm workers in California (right), the huge influx of new immigrants during the 1910s left many native-born Americans fearing the loss of their own jobs. As a result, the United States worked out an agreement with Japan to limit the number of immigrants arriving from that country.

to resent the newcomers, who had foreign languages, customs, and religions. They feared that their own language and traditions might be drowned in a sea of strange new cultures. They were also afraid that the new arrivals would take their jobs away because immigrants were willing to work for lower pay.

Probably the worst example of hostility toward immigrants involved Japanese Americans in California. In October 1906, a San Francisco school board voted to segregate (separate by race) Japanese students, even though only ninety-three out of twenty-five thousand students in San Francisco were Japanese. The Japanese government complained to United States President Theodore Roosevelt when it learned of the situation. Some American politicians were outraged at the Japanese complaint and urged a declaration of war against Japan. To calm the situation and avoid war, President Roosevelt persuaded the school board to end its policy in 1907, after he first worked out a so-called Gentlemen's Agreement with the Japanese government, whereby Japan would no longer allow laborers to immigrate to the United States.

Two Paths to Freedom

During the first decade of the twentieth century, some Americans struggled valiantly to overcome racism—the terrible discrimination that still afflicted the nation almost half a century after the end of slavery. Many immigrant groups were the victims of various forms of discrimination, especially the Chinese and Japanese on the West coast. But those who suffered the most were American Indians and African Americans.

Although both Booker T. Washington (opposite, left) and W.E.B. Du Bois (opposite, right) wanted to improve the lives of their fellow African Americans, they had very different ideas about how to do it. As a result, they viewed each other with great mistrust. One of the most urgent issues for both leaders and all African Americans of the time was lynching (below), which had been going on since the years after the Civil War.

Over the years, mining companies and land speculators had taken away much of the land that had been promised to American Indians by government treaties. Meanwhile, in the South, segregation was the order of the day. Jim Crow laws separated African Americans from whites in almost all public facilities, including schools and rest rooms. Certain laws, such as voting requirements, were also put into place to ensure that African Americans would not be allowed to vote. Even worse, African Americans were often the victims of brutal violence at the hands of white racists. During the 1900s, one hundred African Americans were lynched (killed as punishment for an alleged crime without first having a trial).

Two African-American leaders were determined to fight for equality and an end to discrimination. But these leaders differed in their ideas about the best way to achieve these goals. Booker T. Washington, head of the Tuskegee Institute in Alabama, believed in following the path of least resistance.

He believed that African Americans should first help each other to better themselves economically by becoming educated and starting their own businesses. Only then would African Americans have a good chance of winning social and political equality. W.E.B. Du Bois, on the other hand, believed that African Americans should not wait to struggle for equality. He urged African Americans immediately to demand social equality and the protection of the law against segregation and violence. In 1909, to help further these goals, Du Bois and a group of progressive white and black reformers founded the National Association for the Advancement of Colored People (NAACP).

Where the Jobs Were

America's new role as a global power contributed greatly to an amazing period of growth in the nation's economy. New sources of cheap raw materials were now available to fuel the nation's industries. American corporations also had vast new markets in which to sell and distribute their goods. In such a

All the new businesses needed huge numbers of workers. The list of major corporations founded during the 1900s reads like a Who's Who of corporate America. It includes Firestone Tire, Sylvania Electric, United States Steel, American Can, Quaker Oats, Monsanto Chemical, Philip Morris, J. C. Penney, International Harvester, Pepsi-Cola, Texaco (above), Ford Motor, Continental Can, Bethlehem Steel, Mead Paper, Spiegel Catalog, Gulf Oil, American Cyanimid, Harley-Davidson, General Motors, and McGraw-Hill Books.

favorable economic climate, financing was readily available for the creation of new businesses. Millions of job seekers, foreign immigrants as well as native-born Americans, also helped boost the economy.

Streetcars, Subways, and the Horseless Carriage

New methods of transportation played an important role in the growth of America's cities. People rode electric streetcars to get around town. Often, cities grew up around streetcar routes as they were planned and built. The expansion of Los Angeles was accomplished in such a fashion.

While the streetcar was the most popular means of urban transportation, underground travel also became possible during the 1900s. In New York City, the world's largest subway system was completed in 1904.

But it was the development of the automobile that caused the most excitement during the decade. In 1900, there were about eight thousand registered cars. Fifty manufacturers were selling different forms of the vehicle that was often called the horseless carriage. These vehicles, which were built by hand, cost around one thousand dollars. They were far too expensive for most Americans. That changed when Henry Ford introduced his mass-produced Model T in 1908. The price was $850, well within reach for some middle-class families.

Ten thousand Model T Fords were sold during the first year of production. By decade's end, most of the companies manufacturing horseless carriages at the beginning of the 1900s no longer existed. Because of the enormous technological innovations and price difference, the automobile industry would soon be dominated by Ford, General Motors, and Chrysler.

By 1910, the number of registered cars (above, inset) had climbed to more than 100,000.

In many places, streetcars (above) also connected one city to another. A person could actually travel all the way from New York City to Portland, Maine, by streetcar—a distance of 317 miles!

Fun in the Sun

America's love affair with the automobile was just beginning in the 1900s. During these years, Americans also enjoyed other kinds of rides—specifically, amusement park rides such as the roller coaster. Amusement parks sprang up all across the country and became wildly popular. The parks were easily accessible and affordable, even for working-class Americans.

In New York City, people could ride the streetcar to Coney Island, a resort by the sea, for five cents. Coney Island was home to the world's first roller coaster, known as the

Three separate amusement parks opened at Coney Island during the 1900s—Steeplechase Park, Luna Park, and Dreamland. Steeplechase (above) periodically made visitors an offer they couldn't refuse—twenty-five rides for twenty-five cents. Also popular were expositions and fairs (right). Among them were the 1901 Pan-American Exposition in Buffalo, New York; the 1905 World's Fair at Portland, Oregon; and the 1909 World's Fair at Seattle.

Switchback Railroad. It had opened in 1884. Thrill seekers had a choice of several roller coasters, including the famous Loop the Loop, as well as other types of rides, including a giant Ferris wheel. At Steeplechase Park, visitors lined up to ride mechanical horses that traveled around a circular track high above the park.

Improvements in the Home

During the 1900s, many people lived in cramped tenement apartments with few comforts. Only the wealthy and middle class had indoor plumbing. But changes were afoot that would benefit even working-class Americans.

Electricity was becoming available to more people, making possible the advent of electric household appliances. The electric vacuum cleaner was patented in 1907. At first, only the wealthy could afford one, but eventually, as with other new inventions, the price came down low enough so that almost anyone could afford to buy a vacuum cleaner.

There were many other signs of progress. The icebox provided a practical way to refrigerate food in the home. And thanks to improvements in the canning process, it was no longer necessary for homemakers to can their own food. Canned foods were now available in stores, and even the poor could afford them. Especially popular were the canned products of the Campbell's company.

With the availability of electricity to American homes, new technology quickly became part of everyday life. From sewing machines (above) to vacuum cleaners, improved machinery made household work faster and easier.

Changes in diet came about not only because of canning, but because of a new invention—refrigerated railroad cars (right). With refrigeration, people could easily obtain fresh fruits and vegetables from Florida or California.

In 1904, an artist by the name of Grace Weiderseim designed cartoon characters known as the Campbell's Kids to promote Campbell's soups. The advertising campaign proved so successful that the distinctive red and white Campbell's labels (above, right) she first created were used to sell Campbell's soups not only for the rest of the decade, but the rest of the century.

Probably the most exhausting chore for housewives was the neverending task of washing clothes. During the 1900s, it became possible to send clothes out to laundries. Little by little, some of the drudgery of household chores was being alleviated.

"Milk From Contented Cows"

As a greater variety of household products became available, businesses had to persuade consumers to buy them. Advertising agencies sprang up to spread the word. An effective way of reaching the greatest number of people was through the placing of advertisements in the pages of popular magazines such as the *Saturday Evening Post*. Advertising copywriters came up with catchy phrases. For example, "Milk From Contented Cows" promoted Carnation's dairy products.

Teddy Bear Mania

It all started when President Theodore Roosevelt went on a hunting trip in November 1902. Although he was an experienced hunter, he was not having any luck. So, members of his party caught a young bear and tied it to a tree.

The president, however, refused to shoot it—doing so would have gone against his idea of good sportsmanship. When word of this incident spread, it became the subject of cartoons in the newspapers.

Morris and Rose Mitchom, an enterprising couple who owned a candy store in Brooklyn, New York, began selling a toy bear with moveable body parts. Rose had stitched together the original bear by hand. The Mitchoms received permission from the president to call their product "Teddy's Bear." Because of the publicity about the incident, the bears sold like hotcakes. The Mitchoms could not keep up with the demand, so they teamed up with the Butler Brothers. Together, they started the Ideal Novelty and Toy Company to mass-produce and market their Teddy's Bear, whose name would later be changed to Teddy Bear. The following year, the Teddy Bear craze swept across America. It lasted at least until the end of Roosevelt's second term in office in 1909.

Even today, Americans have a soft spot in their hearts for the cute and cuddly Teddy Bear (below).

The S-Shaped Silhouette

Great Britain's Queen Victoria died on January 22, 1901, but the Victorian influence on fashion in America would continue for most of the 1900s. For women of the upper and middle classes, this meant another decade of formality, characterized by the S-shaped silhouette. This look was achieved by draping a long, bell-shaped skirt over stiff, ruffled petticoats that covered the shoes. At the back, a small, heavy bustle gathered a cloth train. A corset laced as tightly as possible forced a tiny waist and flat stomach while exaggerating the breasts and bustled hips. Completing the look was a high, stiff collar; a wide-brimmed hat; and pointed suede shoes or leather boots fastened with buttons.

By the end of the decade, formality was declining. Women were getting tired of always being uncomfortable. Hemlines rose to the top of the boot, skirts narrowed slightly, corsets no longer reached above the waist, and petticoats were replaced by closer-fitting slips.

Gibson Girls

Another fashion trend had emerged during the 1890s in the illustrations of Charles Dana Gibson, whose work appeared in the pages of *Life* magazine. The Gibson look became increasingly popular with American women during the 1900s. It featured the shirtwaist—a blouse designed to be worn with a high-waisted ankle-length skirt. Young women drawn to the Gibson look often aspired to be secretaries or typists. They favored practical, comfortable, yet stylish clothing that could be worn for everyday activities, especially for work at the office.

Women went to great lengths to achieve the perfect look (below), wearing tight undergarments to force their bodies into the right shape, based on the fashion of the time. Women were known to faint when their corset strings were pulled too tight.

The Gibson girl look became so popular that artists copied it on advertisements, posters, and even sheet music of the time (right).

LOVES GOLDEN STAR

Reverie

by
LOUIS A. DRUMHELLER

(60)

THE MORRIS MUSIC PUB. CO.
PHILADELPHIA, PA.

Except for the rich, most American women had always made their own clothes. But the influx of Jewish and Eastern European tailors led to the growth of the ready-to-wear clothing industry in New York City. During the 1900s, many women bought shirtwaists and other items from the mail-order Sears, Roebuck catalog. By 1905, the catalog offered one hundred fifty different types of shirtwaists.

Bowlers and Boaters

Like women's fashions, men's clothing during the decade was slowly becoming less stiff and formal. Many young men were moving away from the Victorian full beard. They dared to appear in public with just a mustache or even with a totally clean-shaven face. In 1901, middle- and upper-class men typically wore a long frock coat, a waistcoat, and striped trousers to the office. They wore a closely fitted dinner jacket in the evening. By the middle of the decade, young men began wearing a more relaxed lounge suit to the office. A hat was always popular for most occasions, whether it was a silk top hat, a soft felt homburg, a bowler with a rounded top and narrow brim, or a straw hat known as a boater, which was worn in the summer. Other popular accessories included cuff links and pocket watches with long chains.

Although men's fashions (below) relaxed considerably during the first decade of the twentieth century, there was still a long way to go before men could dress casually in public places.

THE JUNGLE
BY
UPTON SINCLAIR

Americans who read *The Jungle* were thoroughly disgusted and horrified. Some were afraid they could never eat meat again. Because of the outcry over contaminated food products, Congress passed two food and drug acts in 1906—the Meat Inspection Act and the Pure Food and Drug Act. These were precursors to the strict laws that govern food production today.

DOUBLEDAY, PAGE & CO
NEW YORK

Muckrakers and Meatpackers

Novelist Upton Sinclair was known as a muckraker, a name given to those who exposed corruption (in other words, raked up the muck) in business or politics. Sinclair had earned the title by writing an exposé of the meatpacking industry in his novel *The Jungle*, published in 1906. The characters in the novel were poor immigrants from Lithuania who worked in Chicago's stockyards and meat-processing plants. Sinclair filled his realistic portrayal with graphic descriptions of the extremely unsanitary practices that were used in the meat industry.

When President Theodore Roosevelt read the book, he was outraged by what was going on in Chicago. He ordered Congress to do something about it. After government investigators confirmed that Sinclair's description was true, Congress passed the Pure Food and Drug Act and the Meat Inspection Act. Roosevelt signed both into law on the same day.

Still, Upton Sinclair was not totally satisfied. He had hoped to improve the lot of poor workers in the meat-processing plants by drawing attention to their awful working conditions as well as the unsanitary practices. Americans, however, were more concerned about their own food. "I aimed for the public's heart and by accident I hit it in the stomach," Sinclair said.

Living through the great San Francisco earthquake (above) was just one of many hair-raising episodes in author Jack London's adventure-filled life. At the age of eighteen, he went to sea on a sealing schooner. At the age of twenty-one, he went to Alaska to seek his fortune in the Klondike gold rush. London used his experiences to write his novels *The Call of the Wild* (1901), *The Sea-Wolf* (1904), and *White Fang* (1906).

"This Night of Terror"

These were the words of writer Jack London. He was referring to the second night of fires devouring San Francisco after a horrifying earthquake on April 18, 1906. On the night of April 19, London was amazed that people were calm and quiet, "while the whole city crashed and roared into ruin." He remarked that the people were kinder and more courteous than at any other time in the city's history. Jack London's amazement was understandable, considering the magnitude of the disaster. At least 3,000 people died, and more than two hundred thousand were left homeless by the earthquake and fires that swept through San Francisco for three days.

Everything Has a Name

Helen Keller had been blind and deaf since she was nineteen months old. When Helen was six, her tutor, Anne Sullivan, taught her how to spell words by tracing the shapes of letters onto Helen's hand. One day, Sullivan wrote "water" on Helen's hand while pouring water from a pump onto Helen's other hand. Only then did Helen grasp that the words she had been spelling were the names of things—and that everything has a name.

Helen soon learned hundreds of words and then learned how to read using Braille, a system of reading for the blind. Helen wrote poems and stories. By the time she was ten, Helen was communicating with sign language. By age sixteen, she had learned to speak by touching people's noses, lips, and throats as they spoke to her. In 1902, Helen became famous when her autobiography, *The Story of My Life*, was published. In 1904, she graduated from Radcliffe College. She was twenty-two years old. She then devoted her time to improving education for the blind and deaf.

The Twelve-Minute Western

Americans had begun viewing moving pictures in the 1890s. While looking into a machine known as a kinetoscope, they turned a crank with their hand. The figures on the tiny screen seemed to come to life before their eyes. But after the novelty wore off, audiences grew tired of the silent newsreels and sight gags that typically lasted about half a minute. Soon, however, movies were about to take a major leap forward.

In 1903, Edwin Porter produced a twelve-minute-long silent film called *The Great Train Robbery*. It was America's first Western movie. Audiences were thrilled to see gunslingers of the Old West galloping across the screen. They were captivated by the conflict between heroes and villains. The public began clamoring for more movies. More Westerns followed, as well as Civil War dramas, crime stories, and comedies. But *The Great Train Robbery* remained the single most popular movie of the decade.

Helen Keller (below, left) is able to "hear" her instructor, Anne Sullivan, by feeling the vibration of her lips as she speaks.

Vaudeville Theaters and Nickelodeons

At first, films were shown as part of the entertainment at vaudeville theaters, between the live acts. Vaudeville entertainment featured singers, dancers, comedians, acrobats, and jugglers. Among the most famous vaudeville entertainers were Bert Williams, an African-American singer and dancer; Eddie Foy, an Irish dancer and pantomimist; comedian Ed Wynn; and singers Sophie Tucker and Al Jolson. There were also novelty acts such as Blatz the Human Fish, who ate, read, and played the trombone under water. Also popular was female impersonator Julian Eltinge, who in 1907 dressed up as "The Simpson Girl," a spoof of the Gibson girl look.

Films were also shown in storefronts. The audience sat on folding chairs in front of a screen. In 1905, a storefront theater that featured comfortable seating and live piano accompaniment opened in Pittsburgh, Pennsylvania. Because the price of admission was a nickel, the theater became

The earliest films were little more than still images shown so rapidly the objects appeared to be moving (below). By the end of decade, films would be much improved.

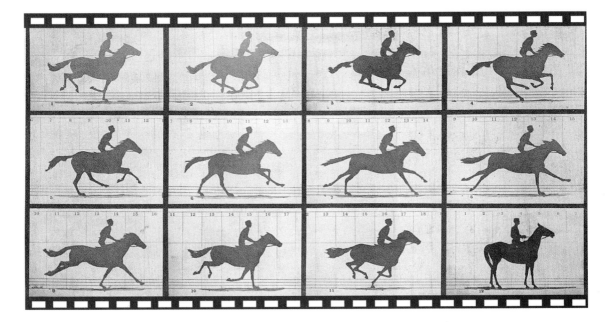

At the time he produced *The Great Train Robbery* (left), Edwin Porter was working as a director and cameraman for the Edison Company, a film production business started by inventor Thomas Alva Edison.

known as a nickelodeon. By 1909, there were more than four thousand nickelodeons in America, and more than 80 million tickets were being sold every week.

Tin Pan Alley

One evening in 1903, a New York City newspaper reporter was strolling down Twenty-eighth Street in Manhattan. When he entered the block between Broadway and Sixth Avenue, he heard a confusion of musical sounds coming at him from open windows on both sides of the street. He was overwhelmed by the effect of clashing melodies and harmonies. Upon investigating the situation, the reporter learned that, up and down the block, the offices were occupied by publishers of sheet music. In each building, songwriters and piano players were hard at work cranking out new songs. The reporter called the street "Tin Pan Alley" because of all the noise.

There was a lot of money to be made from selling sheet music, especially if the songs became popular hits. Music was common entertainment in the homes of many Americans, and many families owned a piano. Phonographs and records were also becoming popular. At first, most recorded music consisted of excerpts from operas, featuring famous singers such as Enrico Caruso. By the end of the decade popular songs eventually found their way onto phonograph records. Among the decade's most popular tunes were "In the Good Old Summertime" (1902), "Meet Me in St. Louis" (1904), and "Give My Regards to Broadway" (1904).

Ragtime

A style of music known as ragtime was especially popular throughout the decade. It had its origins in the 1880s as an African- American musical form featuring syncopated rhythms. The ragtime piano compositions of African-American pianist Scott Joplin became known for their distinctive melodies and rich harmonies. Joplin soon came to be called the Ragtime King. His "Maple Leaf Rag," composed in 1899, became America's most popular piano rag by 1909. However, not everyone in America was fond of ragtime music. In 1901, the American Federation of Musicians passed an anti-ragtime resolution, calling for "every effort to suppress and discourage such musical trash." Despite these efforts, ragtime thrived.

The Birth of the Blues

Since the days of slavery, African-Americans in the South had been singing the blues—songs of sorrow, loneliness, defiance, and humor. The typical format of a blues song was a 12-bar melody with repeats and responses. Ma Rainey (born Gertrude Pridgett), an African-American singer, heard her first blues song in 1902. Ma Rainey performed in minstrel shows, a type of variety entertainment that had been popular since the Civil War. When she began singing blues songs on stage, she became known as the "Mother of the Blues." W.C. Handy, known as the "Father of the Blues," wrote his first blues song in 1909. In the years to come, the blues and ragtime would be the main elements of a new music called jazz.

Composer Scott Joplin (above), perhaps the best-known ragtime musician of the era, was called the Ragtime King. Some of his hits remain popular even today.

Gladiators of the Twentieth Century

As a child, President Theodore Roosevelt had suffered from asthma and spent most of his time indoors. As he grew older, his father encouraged him to participate in strenuous sports such as boxing, swimming, and horseback riding. By doing so, Roosevelt regained his health.

One of Roosevelt's favorite sports was football. He admired aggressive behavior on the playing field. The only problem was that football, especially college football, was extremely brutal during the 1900s. Many young men were killed while playing. Eventually, pressure grew to find a way to make football less dangerous. Some journalists and college presidents were even calling for the game to be abolished.

In 1905, Roosevelt called a football summit before the start of the college football season. He invited athletic officials and presidents of the Ivy League colleges to the White House. Roosevelt thought he could persuade them to "teach men to play football honestly." College football, however, had become a huge commercial

Theodore Roosevelt (above) attributed his dynamic leadership to his sports activities. He was convinced that participation in sports such as football (opposite) was essential to the development of character. His love of sports led him to encourage football reform.

So many young men were killed playing football (above) that the game might have been compared to gladiator combat in the blood-soaked arenas of ancient Rome. Offensive formations, such as the flying wedge, were almost guaranteed to result in serious injury to players, who at times wore no protective gear.

enterprise. Winning meant everything—a college's prestige depended on victory. Training was often haphazard, with punishing schedules. At times, violence was deliberately encouraged.

Very little was accomplished at the White House summit. The delegates promised to "eliminate unnecessary roughness, holding, and foul play." On the playing field, however, nothing changed. During the 1905 season, eighteen players died and 159 were seriously injured. The next year, two organizations— the Intercollegiate Athletic Association (IAA) and the Intercollegiate Rules Committee—joined to make some changes in the rules of the game to reduce the brutality of football. Still, players continued to die. There was no significant drop in the death and injury rate until protective equipment was introduced during the 1910s.

The Birth of the World Series

By 1900, baseball had been popular with American sports lovers for at least a quarter of a century. The National League (NL), in existence since 1876, had eight teams in 1900—Boston, Brooklyn, Chicago, Cincinnati, New York, Philadelphia, Pittsburgh, and St. Louis. Although baseball had been around for quite a while, changes were coming.

In 1900, Byron Bancroft "Ban" Johnson, the president of the minor-league Western Association (WA), announced that he was changing the league's name to the American League (AL). It would now be considered a major league, on the same level as the NL.

At first, NL officials did not take the AL seriously. But once they realized that baseball fans were very interested in the new league, they became concerned. They soon realized that the AL meant trouble for the NL. By 1903, more than one hundred NL players, many of them popular with the fans, had switched to the AL, responding to offers of better salaries.

Something had to be done. In 1903, managers from the two leagues got together and hammered out an agreement called "The Joint Playing Rules." These became the official rules of baseball for both leagues. Then, they scheduled a special baseball event, a "World Series," which would take place at the close of the 1903 baseball season. The champion

During the days of the WA, the NL used to raid the WA teams, scooping up any players who showed promise. Now, with two leagues competing for players (right), the shoe was on the other foot.

teams of each league would play in a five-out-of-nine series. In the 1903 World Series, the NL's Pittsburgh Pirates played against the AL's Boston Pilgrims. To the surprise of the NL, Boston won.

The following year, in 1904, there was no World Series. The NL's champion team, the New York Giants, refused to play Boston, which was once again the AL's champion. Giants manager John McGraw refused to play against what he called a "minor league" club. Perhaps he had another reason—fear of losing. At any rate, baseball fans were disappointed. So, in 1905, both leagues once again held a World Series. This time, it would be a four-out-of-seven series. The New York Giants defeated the AL's Philadelphia Athletics. From now on, the

World Series would be an important annual event, to the delight of baseball fans all across America.

The 1900 Olympic Games

In 1900, the second modern Olympic Games competition was held in Paris, France. (The first modern Games had taken place in 1896, after a break of fifteen hundred years since the last Olympics.) Although many of the athletes from other nations found the behavior of the American team somewhat loud and rude—the French called the Americans *sauvages* (savages)—the Games were marked by a friendly and warm spirit of sportsmanship.

The United States athletes dominated the Games in track and field events, particularly in sprints. Among the big winners was American J.W.B. Tewksbury, who ran to victory in the 200-meter dash. Strangely, University of Pennsylvania student Tewksbury and many of his teammates did not realize that the competition was, in fact, the Olympics until they were handed medals!

At forty-two, Theodore Roosevelt was the youngest person ever to become president of the United States. Roosevelt's experience with the Rough Riders during the Spanish-American War helped prepare him to become one of the United States' most powerful and influential presidents. Roosevelt is seen wearing his Rough Riders uniform.

Theodore Roosevelt: Rough Rider

On September 6, 1901, President William McKinley was assassinated while attending the Pan-American Exposition in Buffalo, New York. He was shot by Leon Czolgosz, a man claiming to be an anarchist (someone who opposes all government). Vice President Theodore Roosevelt became president, and began a period of presidential politics known as the Progressive Era, which would last for almost two decades. The forty-two-year-old Republican president was eager to tackle difficult challenges and to accomplish great things.

Roosevelt had previously served as a New York state assemblyman. In the assembly, he had stood up to wealthy railroad owner Jay Gould and had sponsored legislation to improve the working conditions of New York City cigar makers. Later, as a New York City police commissioner, he worked to clean up a corrupt city police force.

In 1896, Roosevelt was appointed assistant secretary of the navy by President McKinley. At that time, Cubans were trying to win their freedom from Spain. Roosevelt was in favor of helping the Cubans. Because McKinley did not want to risk war with Spain, the outspoken Roosevelt declared that McKinley had "no more backbone than a chocolate eclair."

Many people of the time were so outraged by President McKinley's assassination that he was declared "martyred." This picture (right) originally appeared in a biography about the fallen president, in which Leon Czolgosz was referred to as the "dastardly assassin."

War finally did break out between the United States and Spain in February 1898, after the American battleship *Maine* blew up in a Cuban harbor.

Roosevelt left his navy job and volunteered for the army. He trained for a month with a one-thousand-man regiment made up of cowboys, frontiersmen, and an assortment of sportsmen, who became known as Roosevelt's Rough Riders. In Cuba, he led his troops against the Spaniards in a famous charge up San Juan Hill, near the city of Santiago. Also taking part in the battle was the 10th cavalry regiment of African-American troops. Roosevelt regarded his experience at San Juan Hill as "the great day of my life."

The Spanish-American War of 1898 was over in just six months. The victorious United States won control of the former Spanish possessions of Cuba and Puerto Rico in the Caribbean, and the Philippines, Guam, and Wake Island in the Pacific. Later that year, Roosevelt, now considered a war hero, was elected governor of New York. Two years later, the Republicans chose him as McKinley's vice presidential running mate in

Roosevelt (above) and his boundless energy seemed to reflect the dynamic changes under way in America. His optimism seemed to embody the view that the twentieth century would indeed be an American century.

The Northern Securities Company owned by J. P. Morgan (above) consisted of the major railroads linking the Great Lakes with the Pacific coast. When President Roosevelt broke it up, his reputation as a trustbuster was born. By the end of Roosevelt's second term, the government had taken forty-three trusts to court.

the election of 1900. After McKinley's assassination, President Roosevelt, the enthusiastic Rough Rider, was ready for new battles. He was ready to fight the trusts.

Trustbusting

The purpose of the Sherman Antitrust Act of 1890 was to prevent businesses from joining together in ways that would restrain trade or commerce. Unfortunately, the government did not enforce the act. The most powerful corporations in industries such as railroads, aluminum, tobacco, life insurance, sugar, and coal gobbled up weaker competitors and merged with strong competitors to form huge monopolies known as trusts.

In 1900, President McKinley had campaigned against the trusts. He said they were "dangerous conspiracies against the public good" and that they should be regulated by law. Theodore Roosevelt agreed. In his first State of the Union Address, he argued that, because the trusts did business in many states, they could not be regulated by state law. The federal government had to "assume the power of supervision and regulation over all corporations doing an interstate business."

The arrogant attitude and blatant disregard for the public good shown by one of America's wealthiest men, John Pierpont (J. P.) Morgan, particularly infuriated Roosevelt. Morgan had once commented, "I owe the public nothing."

He explained that it was his duty to bring rival companies together in a trust for their mutual benefit. He claimed to want to make business more rational and efficient. Many of his critics, however, believed he and his associates were instead working to cheat the public. In 1902, the Roosevelt administration brought a suit under the Sherman Antitrust Act to dissolve the Northern Securities Company, a transportation monopoly controlled by Morgan.

In 1903, Congress agreed to Roosevelt's proposal to create the Department of Commerce and Labor, including a Bureau of Corporations to investigate possible violations of antitrust law. In 1904, the Supreme Court ordered that Northern Securities be dissolved. When William Howard Taft, Roosevelt's handpicked successor, became president in 1909, he continued the antitrust suits brought by Roosevelt. Indeed, Taft would prove to be an even more effective trustbuster than Roosevelt.

William Howard Taft (below) was groomed by Theodore Roosevelt to succeed him to the presidency. By helping to elect his own successor, Roosevelt hoped to see the policies he began continued through the next administration.

Roosevelt: Labor Negotiator

In 1902, Theodore Roosevelt became the first president to mediate a labor dispute. About one hundred fifty thousand mine workers in the Northeast, led by John Mitchell, president of the United Mine Workers (UMW), went on strike for better pay, a shorter workday, and recognition of their union. During the next few months, the price of coal skyrocketed as

As president, Theodore Roosevelt set several precedents. In 1901, about a month after becoming president, Roosevelt outraged Southern white Democrats by inviting African-American leader Booker T. Washington to dinner at the White House. Roosevelt is seen (above) with a group of coal miners during the strike he helped settle.

supplies dwindled. With winter approaching, Roosevelt was determined to take action to end the strike.

The mine owners had refused to negotiate with the union. They demanded that Roosevelt send in troops to crush the strike. By this time, most of the American public sympathized with the miners. Angered by the mine owners' stubbornness, Roosevelt threatened to send in the army, not to attack the miners, but to seize and operate the mines. This sent the mine owners scurrying to the negotiating table, and the five-month-long anthracite coal strike was called off. At the mediation session in Scranton, Pennsylvania, both sides agreed to a 10 percent pay increase for the miners and a nine-hour workday.

The Square Deal

When Roosevelt ran for another term in office in 1904, he promised Americans a "Square Deal." Mindful of Roosevelt's intervention in the coal strike and his breakup of Northern Securities, many believed in his sense of fairness. Americans also responded favorably when Roosevelt advocated the conservation of natural resources on public land, becoming the first president to do so. Believing Roosevelt had their best interests at heart, Americans voted him into office for a full term of his own.

A First Time for Everything

In 1906, Roosevelt became the first president to win the Nobel peace prize for his role as mediator in helping to end the 1904–1905 war between Russia and Japan. In 1906, Roosevelt traveled to Panama to see for himself how the Panama Canal

Theodore Roosevelt won the Nobel Prize for his efforts in ending the Russo-Japanese War. He is seen here (below) during the negotiations with the Russian and Japanese diplomats.

project was progressing, thus becoming the first president to take a trip abroad. In 1910, the year after he left office, Roosevelt, looking for new adventures, went for a ride in a plane built by the Wright brothers.

"Speak Softly and Carry a Big Stick"

These words, a West African proverb, summed up the policies of President Theodore Roosevelt. He believed that a policy based on persuasive diplomacy backed by military might was the best way to get things done. Time and again, Roosevelt followed this principle in his dealings with the nations of the Caribbean and Latin America. In 1902, by announcing that the United States Navy was ready to go into action, he persuaded Germany, Great Britain, and Italy to negotiate with Venezuela over the payment of debts rather than intervene militarily.

Building a Canal

In 1903, the United States wanted to build a canal across Panama, which was then a province of Colombia. For many years, the only ways to travel by water from the Atlantic to the Pacific were to either sail around the tip of South America, or to sail to Central America, cross overland, and then take another ship on the Pacific side. A canal would dramatically shorten the trip by providing ships with a water route through Central America.

President Roosevelt made a special trip to see the progress of the digging of the Panama Canal (left, the president can be seen sitting on a digging machine and wearing a white suit).

In the process of building the Panama canal (above), countless lives were lost due to accident and disease.

Colombia did not agree to the United States' proposal to build a canal, however. Encouraged by the United States, Panamanians made plans to secede from (leave) Colombia. When Colombia sent troops to stop the Panamanians, United States Navy ships prevented them from landing. The United States government recognized Panama's independence, and a grateful Panama gave the United States a ten-mile-wide strip of land across Panama on which to build a canal. Construction on the fifty-one-mile-long Panama Canal began shortly after the signing of the agreement between the two countries. It would take ten years to complete before it opened in 1914.

The Russo-Japanese War and the 1905 Revolution

President Roosevelt was eager to project American power and influence to more distant parts of the world as well as Latin America. In September 1905, he mediated an end to the war between Russia and Japan, the nation that was becoming America's chief rival in the Pacific. The war had begun in February 1904, after tensions between the two nations had reached a boiling point. Each wanted control over Korea and Chinese Manchuria, but it soon became clear that victory was beyond the grasp of either power, although much smaller Japan was able to humiliate the great Russian Empire by sinking many of its ships.

Russia's leader, Tsar Nicholas II, also had to deal with a revolution that swept through Russia in 1905. On January 22, 1905, a day that would become known as Bloody Sunday, some two hundred thousand Russians, mainly poor working people, marched peacefully through St. Petersburg. They had taken to the streets to plead with the tsar for better working and living conditions. Tsar Nicholas's soldiers met the marchers with a sudden hail of gunfire, killing hundreds of men, women, and children, and wounding thousands more.

The 1905 rebellion by outraged citizens spread throughout Russia. Millions of striking workers brought the nation to a standstill. In his October Manifesto, Nicholas II agreed to grant the Russian people civil rights, including an elected lawmaking body called the Duma. After the revolution ended, however,

Nicholas failed to live up to his promises. He dissolved the Duma when it dared to challenge his policies.

The Great White Fleet

In 1907, Theodore Roosevelt sent the "Great White Fleet," a group of sixteen United States battleships so named because of their color, on a forty-three-thousand-mile world tour. Among the places the fleet visited were Japan, China, and Australia. The tour was designed to show the world the terrific naval power of the

United States and to intimidate those nations that might consider challenging American interests abroad. As a result of the fleet's trip, the United States and Japan signed a new agreement spelling out their mutual interests in the Pacific Ocean. Japan was permitted to keep Korea in return for recognizing American rule over the Philippines, which the United States had won from Spain in the Spanish-American War of 1898.

Nicholas II (bottom left) would be the last of the Russian tsars. Despite his concessions to the people when he created the Duma after the 1905 revolution (left), Russians would continue to demand more changes. Eventually, Communist revolutionaries would overthrow the government and set up the Soviet Union.

American battleships (left) were sent on a journey around the world to demonstrate the mighty naval power of the United States. The fleet's trip was a bold statement of President Roosevelt's motto, "Speak softly and carry a big stick." Roosevelt's efforts would help make the United States one of the strongest nations in the world.

The historic flight of the Wright brothers (above) would change the world forever. Of course, men had flown earlier in gliders without motors. In 1896, Octave Chanute had flown 256 feet along the Indiana shore of Lake Michigan in a two-winged glider. The Wright brothers succeeded where others had failed because they solved the problem of the interaction between wing and air currents. Other inventors had focused mainly on the engine. In 2003, the Wright Brothers Flying bi-wing was recreated (opposite) in honor of the 100th anniversary of their invention.

Learning to Fly

Since the beginning of time, people had entertained the idea of someday flying through the air. After thousands of years, that fantasy finally became a reality in the first decade of the twentieth century.

On December 17, 1903, at Kitty Hawk, North Carolina, Orville Wright made the first powered flight in a heavier-than-air flying machine he had built with his brother, Wilbur. The flight in the "aeroplane," as they called their machine, lasted all of twelve seconds. Orville flew 120 feet, at an average speed of 30 miles per hour. The brothers made several other flights that day, one lasting 59 seconds and covering 852 feet.

Orville Wright was not the first person to travel in the air, although he was the first to fly successfully in a heavier-than-air motor-driven flying machine. Others before had attempted to fly gliders with motors but had failed. Samuel Langley had experimented with unmanned motor-driven model airplanes, flying a model with a one-horsepower steam engine for one thousand feet along the Potomac River in 1903. Also in 1903, two months before Orville Wright's flight, Charles Manly, attempting to fly an airplane with a five-cylinder engine, had to be pulled from the Potomac River after a crash.

People had also been rising into the sky for many years in balloons, which are lighter-than-air crafts. By 1859, at least three thousand balloon ascents had occurred. In 1900, the first flight of a navigable airship, known as a zeppelin, took place at Lake Constance in Germany. In 1905, Roy Knabenshue flew a sixty-two-foot dirigible over New York City. With the Wright brothers' success, however, a new era of air travel had begun. Whether in an airplane or a dirigible, more people would be able to have a bird's-eye view of the earth below.

Although Congress believed in Peary's success, there remain skeptics even today. Historians continue to debate whether it was Peary or Frederick A. Cook (right), another explorer who claimed to have reached the pole weeks before Peary, who actually was the first to the North Pole.

The North Pole—"Mine at Last!"

On April 6, 1909, American Commander Robert Edwin Peary became the first person to reach the North Pole. In his log, he wrote, "The Pole at last. . . . My dream and goal for twenty years. Mine at last!" It had been a long campaign, involving six earlier expeditions that had failed to reach the pole for one reason or another. The seventh and final expedition left New York on July 6, 1908.

When Peary reached the North Pole, the sky was overcast. To verify that he had indeed reached the pole, Peary needed to take readings of the position of the sun. He traveled to a point ten miles away, where the sky was clear. There, he made readings of the altitude of the sun with his instruments. He then backtracked to another point eight miles away and again took readings. He did this several times, wandering back and forth across the pole. In his log, he wrote, "I had for all practical purposes passed over the point where north and

Robert Peary (above) and his crew sailed aboard the Roosevelt, named for the president who was an enthusiastic supporter of polar exploration. President Roosevelt was on hand to bid farewell to the expedition. As the ship sailed away, Peary's navigator waved to the president and shouted, "It's the pole or bust this time, Mr. President!"

south and east and west blend into one." When Peary's claim to discovering the North Pole was finally accepted, after some initial skepticism was laid to rest, Peary was promoted to the rank of rear admiral by Congress in 1911.

Too Hot to Handle: Radium

Marie Curie (right), born Maria Sklodowska in Poland in 1867, had always been interested in science. After getting a degree in physics at the Sorbonne University in Paris, she married a young scientist named Pierre Curie. In 1911, Marie Curie received her second Nobel Prize. This time, it was awarded for chemistry, for isolating radium and successfully studying its chemical properties. In 1914, Marie Curie helped found the Radium Institute in Paris, where she focused her research on the chemistry of radioactive substances and their applications for medicine.

Upon learning of Henri Becquerel's discovery of mysterious rays given off by the element uranium, scientist Marie Curie decided to find out more about it. She called the unknown "X" rays "radiation." Upon experimenting with samples of uranium and pitchblende (a mineral), she discovered that pitchblende was far more radioactive than uranium. She and her husband, Pierre, discovered two new elements in the pitchblende—polonium, named after Marie's native Poland,

and radium. In 1903, Marie Curie became the first woman to be awarded a Nobel Prize. She shared the Nobel Prize in physics with her husband and Henri Becquerel.

Pierre Curie died suddenly in 1906. Marie Curie became the first woman to teach at the Sorbonne (a French university) when she was appointed to the professorship left vacant by the death of her husband. Continuing with her research, she found that radium could be used in the form of X-rays to reveal a picture of the interior of the body. It could also be used to destroy diseased cells.

In 1934, Marie Curie died of leukemia caused by her long exposure to radiation. Sadly, in all the years she had studied uranium and radium, she never connected her own illnesses, nor those of her late husband and her assistants, with the radioactive properties of those substances. After Marie Curie's death, the Radium Institute was renamed the Curie Institute. Her notebooks, in which she recorded all her findings, are still locked up to this day—they are too radioactive to handle!

This famous caricature of the Curies, "Radium," first ran in the popular British periodical *Vanity Fare.*

When the Bell Rings

In 1904, Ivan Pavlov, a scientist in St. Petersburg, Russia, won the Nobel Prize in physiology for his studies of digestion. He had been experimenting with dogs, noticing the way they would salivate or drool when they saw food. He said that this was a natural reflex, because dogs needed saliva to help digest food. Pavlov began ringing a bell whenever he brought food to the dogs. They drooled when they saw the food. Then Pavlov rang the bell without bringing food. He saw that the dogs drooled anyway. Pavlov realized that they drooled because they associated the bell with the food. He called this response a conditioned reflex.

Typhoid Mary

Mary Mallon, an immigrant from Ireland, was a prisoner in New York City. But she was no ordinary prisoner. She had committed no crime and she was not locked up in jail. For three years, from 1907 to 1910, Mallon was held in Riverside Hospital in the Bronx, New York. She was considered a threat to public health.

Earlier in the decade, Mallon had caught typhoid fever. When she recovered, she went back to her job as a cook for wealthy families on Long Island. Family members in seven of the eight families for whom she had worked were struck with typhoid fever. Apparently, people who had already recovered from the disease were capable of infecting others, even though they themselves were no longer sick. Mallon was one such person. George Soper, a health worker, managed to trace the spread of the disease back to her. The bacteria, salmonella typhi, was passed from one person to another by people who had caught typhoid fever. Handling food was an easy way to transmit the bacteria to other people. Mallon was directly responsible for fifty-three cases, including three deaths, and up to another fourteen hundred cases in Ithaca, New York, in 1903. After disappearing for several years, following her release in 1910, Mallon was located in 1914 and imprisoned in the hospital again. This time, she was held until the day she died, in 1938.

Food handling, which Mary Mallon (above) did for a living, was an easy way to spread germs—especially in the often unsanitary kitchens of the 1900s.

An Amazing Decade

The 1900s marked the beginning of a new era, which was destined to be considered by many the American century. The enormous flow of immigrants was quickly changing the face of the United States from a predominantly rural country to one with booming cities.

President Theodore Roosevelt, in 1901, ushered in two decades of progressive politics. Known as a trustbuster, Roosevelt was determined to have the government regulate corporate behavior, at least in instances where excessive greed on the part of powerful industrialists threatened public welfare. Roosevelt also became the first president to end a major strike by mediating a labor dispute. Roosevelt's administration was not always kindhearted, however. Roosevelt used the threat of military force to achieve his goals in Latin America and in other parts of the world. Other nations were given notice that, in the twentieth century, the United States would be a major player on the world stage.

No other place on Earth could compare to America in the opportunities it offered for a better life. Technological change picked up speed with the spread of electricity and increasing numbers of automobiles, not to mention the advent of such marvels as flying machines. Lifestyles started to become easier, allowing Americans more time to enjoy themselves at activities such as bike riding (opposite).

Timeline

1900—A wave of immigration continues, during which some 9 million people will move to the United States before 1910; The minor league Western Association becomes the major league **American League**; **William McKinley** is elected president in November, with **Theodore Roosevelt** as his vice president; First flight of a zeppelin takes place in Germany.

1901—On January 22, Great Britain's **Queen Victoria** dies; Pan-American Exposition takes place in Buffalo, New York, where President William McKinley is assassinated on September 6; Vice President **Theodore Roosevelt** becomes president; Roosevelt invites African-American leader **Booker T. Washington** to the White House.

1902—Roosevelt becomes the first president to mediate a labor dispute; **Teddy Bear** is introduced after President Roosevelt goes on a failed hunting trip in Mississippi in November; "In the Good Old Summertime" is released; Roosevelt administration begins its trustbusting by bringing suit to dissolve the **Northern Securities Company**; By announcing that the United States Navy is ready to act, Roosevelt persuades Germany, Great Britain, and Italy to negotiate with Venezuela over a debt crisis; The United States grants **Cuba** independence.

1903—Edwin Porter produces **The Great Train Robbery**, the first Western movie; The Joint Playing Rules of baseball are introduced; The first **World Series** takes place at the end of the baseball season, in which the American League Boston Pilgrims beat the National League Pittsburgh Pirates; Congress creates the **Department of Commerce and Labor**; United States urges Panamanian revolution in Colombia in order to win rights to a canal zone; In December, the **Wright brothers** make the world's first heavier-than-air powered flight in an airplane; **Marie Curie** becomes the first woman to win a Nobel Prize; Jack London's **The Call of the Wild** is published.

1904—In February, **Russo-Japanese War** begins; Roosevelt runs for another term in office, promising Americans a Square Deal; World's largest

subway system is completed in **New York City**; World's fair takes place in St. Louis, Missouri; **Grace Weiderseim** designs **Campbell's Kids** for soup cans; Jack London's **The Sea-Wolf** is published; "Meet Me in St. Louis" and "Give My Regards to Broadway" are released; United States Supreme Court dissolves Northern Securities Company.

1905—On January 22, a revolution begins in **Russia** that results in the creation of the Duma; Roosevelt becomes the first president to travel in a submarine; Roosevelt also becomes the first president to win the **Nobel peace prize** for his role in ending the Russo-Japanese War; World's fair is held in Portland, Oregon; A storefront theater becomes the first **nickelodeon**; President Roosevelt calls a football summit to decrease the dangerous violence of the sport; Second World Series is held, in which the New York Giants defeat the Philadelphia Athletics.

1906—On April 18, the **San Francisco earthquake occurs**, killing hundreds and destroying huge amounts of property; Roosevelt travels to **Panama** to oversee work on the canal; San Francisco school board votes to segregate Japanese students in October; Upton Sinclair's **The Jungle** is published; Jack London's **White Fang** is published; "I'm a Yankee Doodle Dandy" is released; United States puts down a Cuban rebellion.

1907—Roosevelt's Gentlemen's Agreement settles a crisis over Japanese immigration to America; Electric vacuum cleaner is patented; Roosevelt sends **Great White Fleet** on a tour around the world to show other nations American naval power; Mary Mallon, also known as **Typhoid Mary**, is taken prisoner to protect the public health.

1908—**Henry Ford** introduces the mass-produced **Model T**; "Take Me Out to the Ball Game" and "Shine On Harvest Moon" are released; **William Howard Taft** is elected president.

1909—**World's fair** is held in Seattle, Washington; "By the Light of the Silvery Moon" is released; "Maple Leaf Rag" is the most popular piano rag tune; On April 6, **Robert Peary** reaches the North Pole.

Further Reading

Books

Evans, Harold. *The American Century*. New York: Alfred A. Knopf, 1998.

Immell, Myra. *The 1900s*. San Diego, Calif.: Greenhaven Press, 2000.

Jennings, Peter, and Todd Brewster. *The Century*. New York: Doubleday, 1998.

Junior Chronicle of the 20th Century. New York: DK Publishing, 1997.

Old, Wendie C. *The Wright Brothers: Inventors of the Airplane*. Berkeley Heights, N.J.: Enslow Publishers, Inc., 2000.

Internet Addresses

Great White Fleet
http://www.greatwhitefleet.org/

The Jungle *by Upton Sinclair*
http://sunsite.berkeley.edu/Literature/Sinclair/TheJungle/

The Wright Stuff
http://www.pbs.org/wgbh/amex/wright/index.html

Theodore Roosevelt
http://www.whitehouse.gov/history/presidents/tr26.html

Index

Morgan, John Pierpont (J. P.),
40–41
muckrakers, 23

N

National Association for the
Advancement of Colored
People (NAACP), 11
National League (NL), 33–34
New York City, 12, 13, 21, 27,
33, 37, 52, 53, 56
New York Giants, 34
Nicholas II, tsar of Russia, 47–48
nickelodeon, 26–27
Northern Securities Company, 41
North Pole, 53–54

O

October Manifesto, 47
Olympic Games (1900), 35

P

Panama Canal, 43–44, 45–46
Pan-American Exposition (1901),
14, 37
Pavlov, Ivan, 55
Peary, Robert Edwin, 53–54
Philadelphia Athletics, 34
Philippines, 38, 49
phonograph, 28
Pittsburgh Pirates, 34
Porter, Edwin, 25
Progressive Era, 37, 59

R

racism, 9–10
ragtime, 28–29

Rainey, Ma ("Mother of the
Blues"), 29
Roosevelt, Theodore, 9, 16–17,
23, 31, 37, 38, 40, 41, 42,
43, 44, 47, 48, 53, 59
Russia, 43, 47–48
Russo-Japanese War, 43, 47

S

San Francisco, California, 9, 24
San Francisco earthquake (1906),
24
Saturday Evening Post, 16
Sea-Wolf, The, 24
sheet music, 27–28
Sherman Antitrust Act, 40–41
"Shine On Harvest Moon", 28
Sinclair, Upton, 23
Sklodowska, Maria. *See* Curie,
Marie.
slavery, 9
Soper, George, 57
Soviet Union, 49
Spain, 37–38, 49
Spanish-American War, 37–38,
49
Square Deal, 42–43
Steeplechase Park, 14
streetcars, 12, 13
subway, 12
Sullivan, Anne, 24

T

"Take Me Out to the Ball
Game", 28
Teddy Bear, 16–17

Tewksbury, J.W.B., 35
"Tin Pan Alley", 27
trustbusting, 40–41
Tucker, Sophie, 26
Tuskegee Institute, 10
Typhoid Mary. *See* Mallon, Mary.

U

United Mine Workers (UMW),
41–42
United States Congress, 23, 41,
52, 54
United States Navy, 44, 46,
48–49
United States Supreme Court, 41
uranium, 54

V

vaudeville, 26
Victoria, queen of England, 17

W

Washington, Booker T., 10–11, 42
Weiderseim, Grace, 16
Western Association (WA), 33, 34
Western movies, 25
White Fang, 24
Williams, Bert, 26
World Series, 33–35
world's fairs, 14
Wright brothers, 44, 51–52
Wynn, Ed, 26

X

X-rays, 54–55

Z

zeppelin, 52

DATE DUE

SEP 1 7 2014

GAYLORD   PRINTED IN U.S.A.